zendoodle color

Inspiring Zendalas

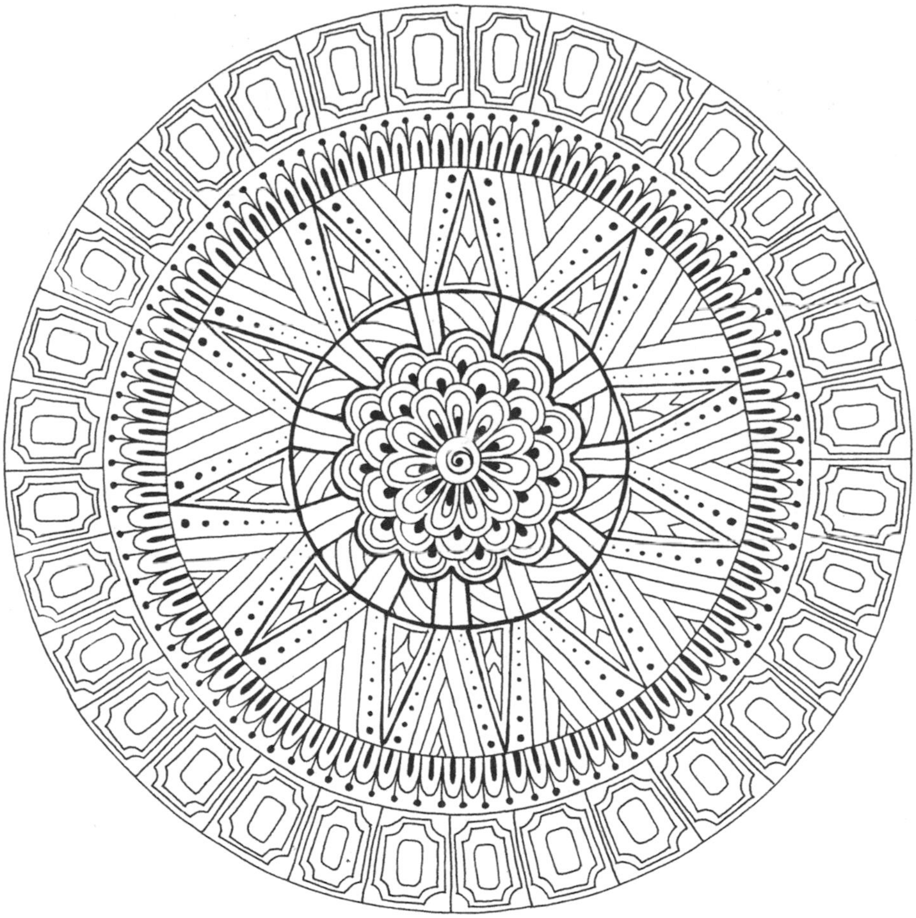

Other great books in the series

zendoodle coloring

Calming Swirls

Creative Sensations

Enchanting Gardens

zendoodle coloring

Inspiring Zendalas

Mystical Circles to Color and Display

Illustrations by

Julia Snegireva

ST. MARTIN'S GRIFFIN
NEW YORK

ZENDOODLE COLORING: INSPIRING ZENDALAS.

Printed in the United States of America. For information, address
St. Martin's Press, 175 Fifth Avenue, New York, N.Y. 10010.

www.stmartins.com

ISBN 978-1-250-08647-1 (trade paperback)

St. Martin's Griffin books may be purchased for educational, business, or promotional use. For information on bulk purchases, please contact the Macmillan Corporate and Premium Sales Department at 1-800-221-7945, extension 5442, or write to specialmarkets@macmillan.com.

First Edition: July 2015

10 9 8 7 6 5 4 3 2 1

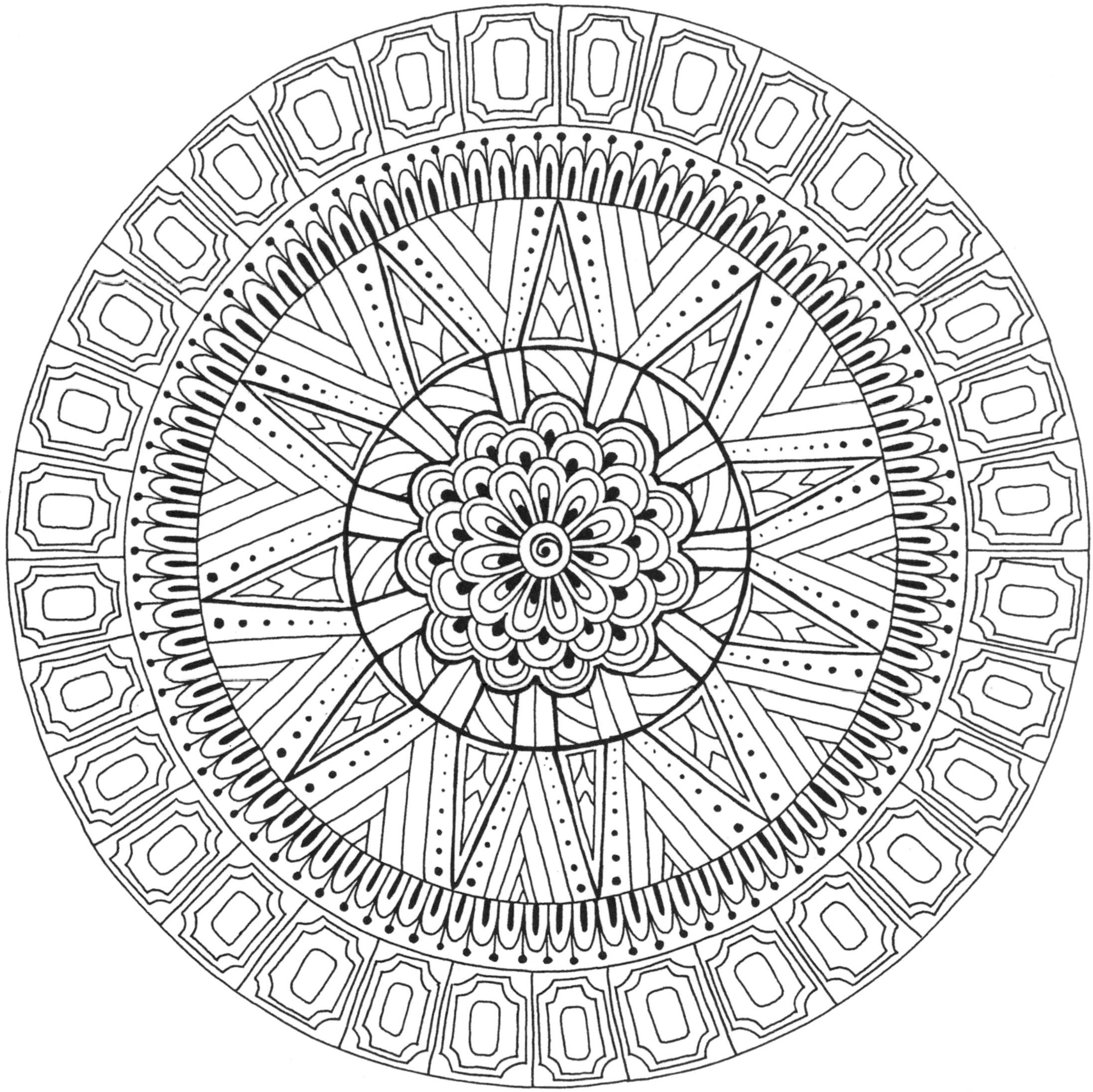

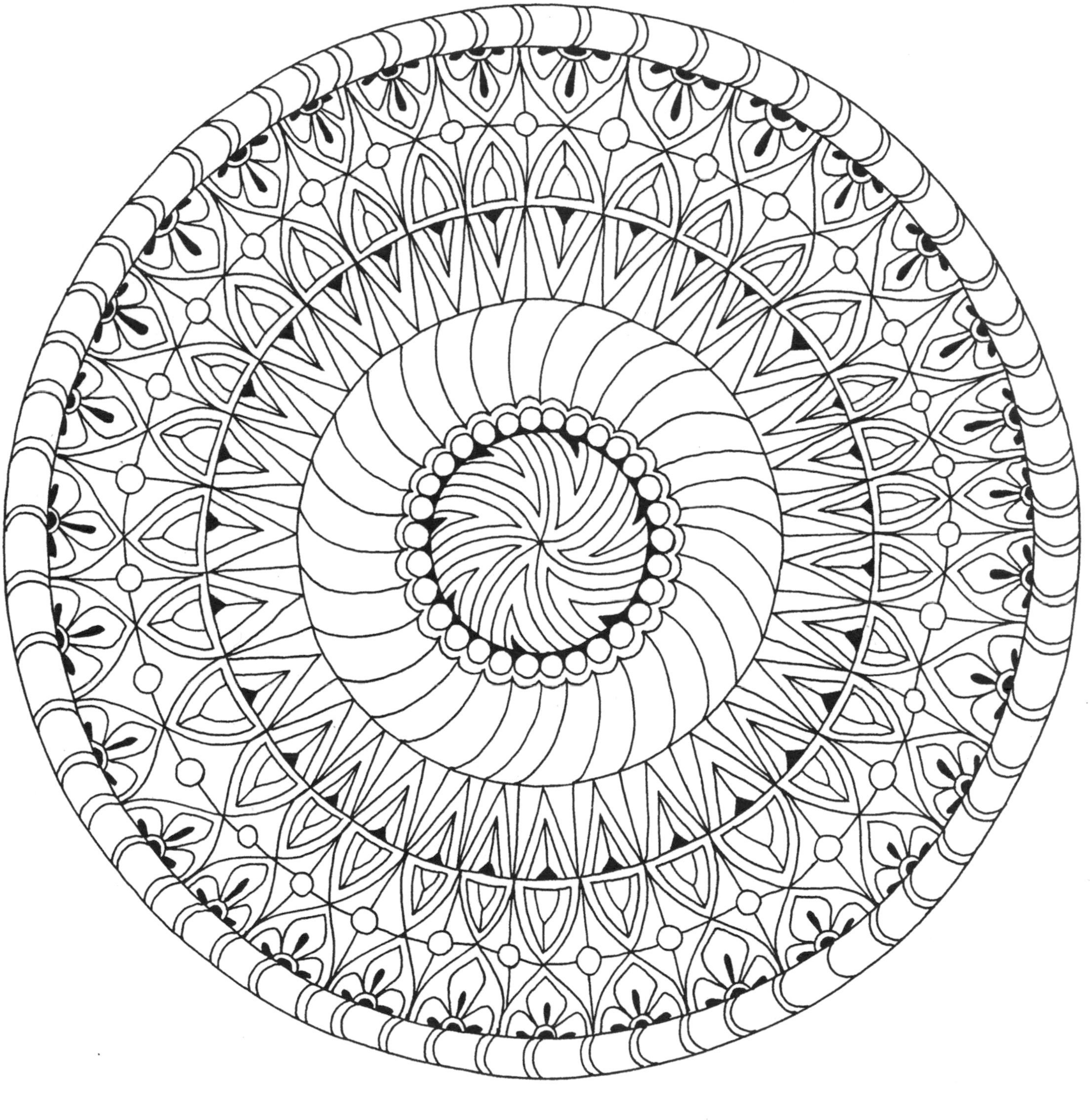

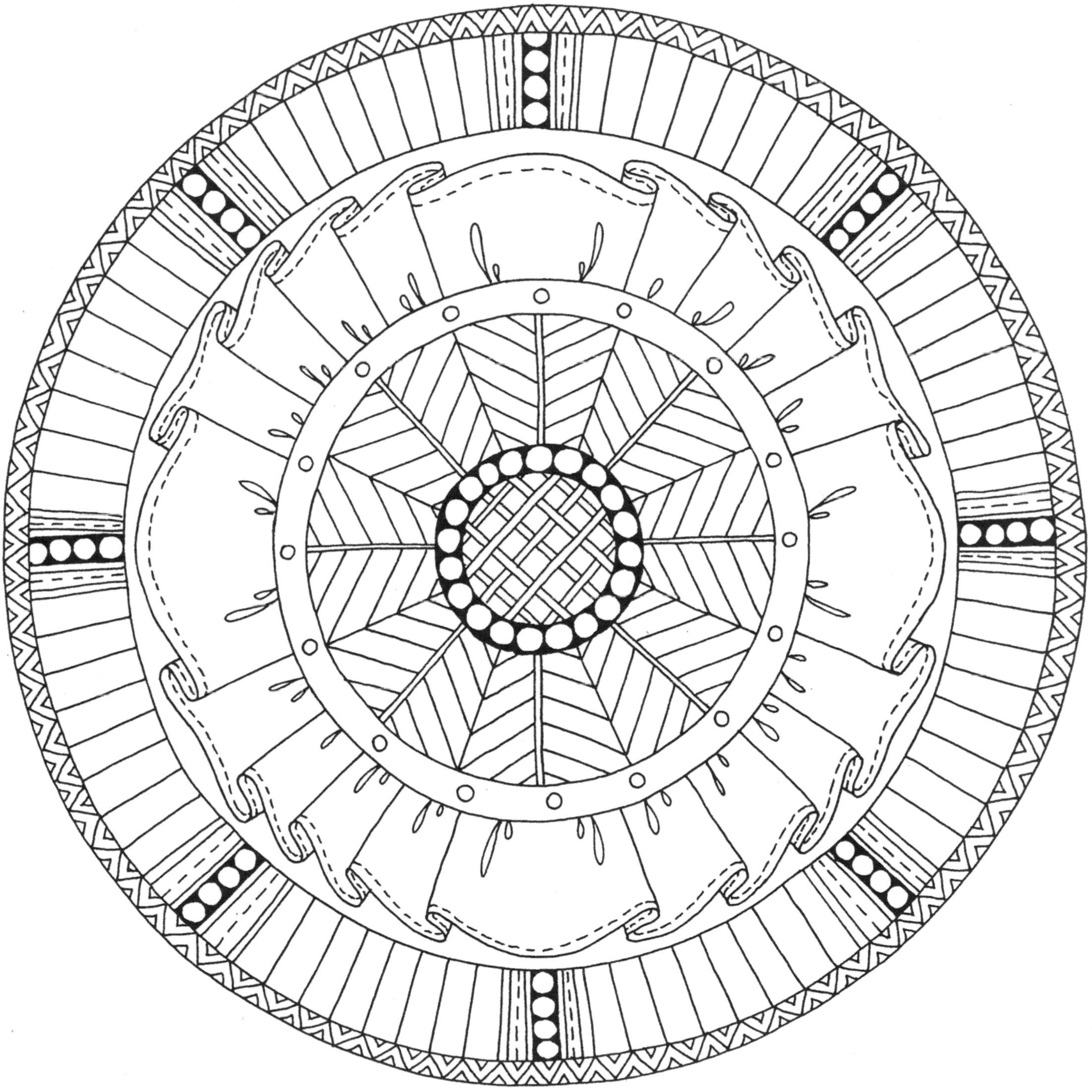

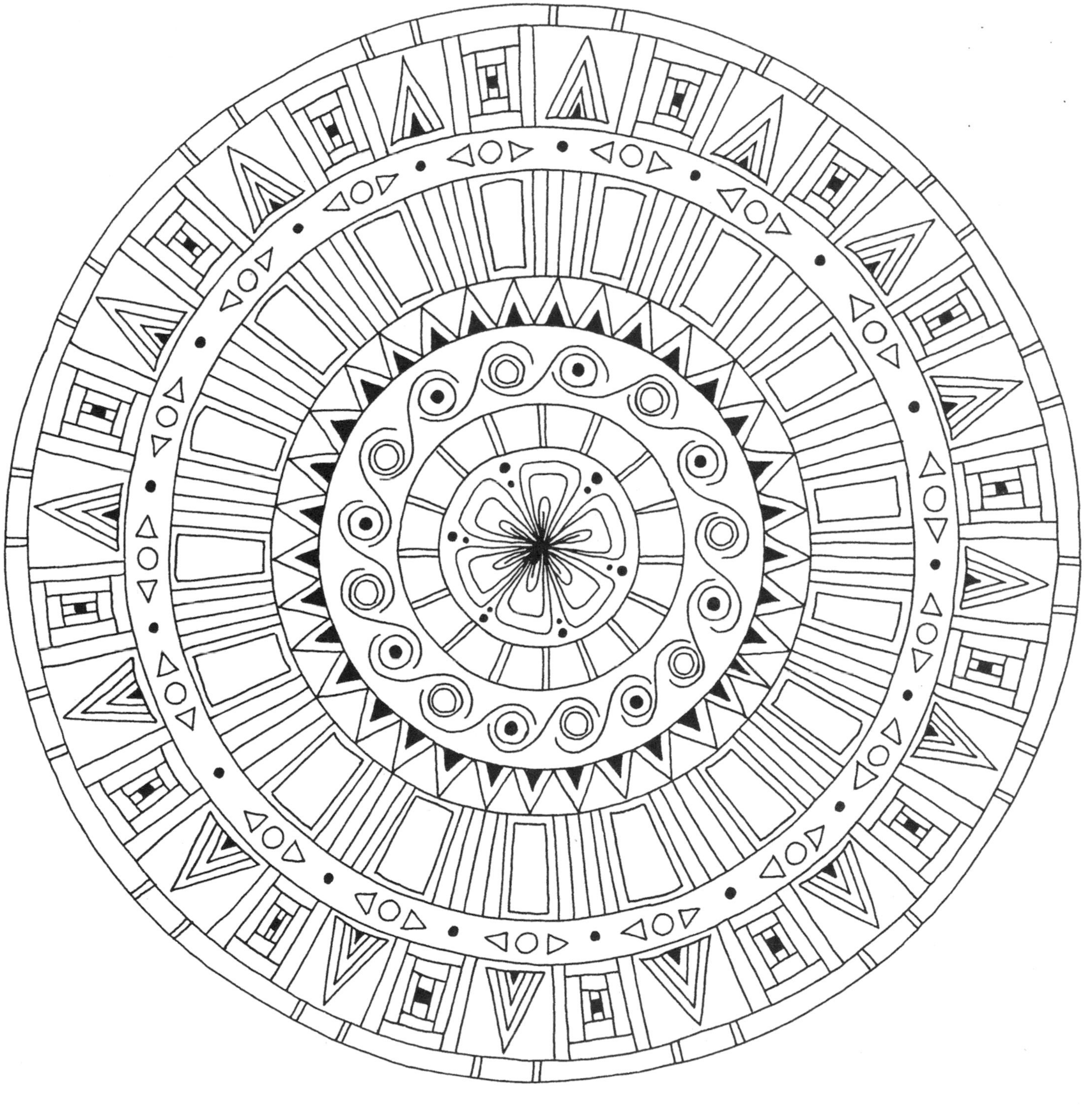